Laugh Together, Stay Together

15 Ways to Lighten Up and Keep Connected

Susanne M. Alexander,
Cool Coach for Couples
with Randy Glasbergen, Cartoonist Extraordinaire

Laugh Together, Stay Together
Published by Marriage Transformation LLC
www.marriagetransformation.com

Printed in the United States of America

ISBN: 978-1-940062-03-7

© 2014 Marriage Transformation LLC. All international rights reserved for the book as a whole. No part of this book may be reproduced by any mechanical, photographic, or electronic process, or by any other means, in the form of a photographic or digital recording, nor may it be stored in a retrieval system, transmitted, or otherwise copied for public or private use, including on the Internet, or re-sold, without the written permission of Marriage Transformation, except by a reviewer, who may quote brief passages in a review. Translations into other languages require permission. Use of the cartoons requires permission from Marriage Transformation and from the cartoonist, who may also charge a licensing fee. Thank you for respecting these legal guidelines. Your integrity with this process spreads a spirit of loving respect throughout the world and makes us very happy.

This publication is intended to provide helpful, fun, and educational information for couples. It is sold with the understanding that the publisher and the author are not engaged in rendering legal or clinical advice. No information, advice, or suggestions by the author are intended to take the place of directly consulting with a therapist or licensed professional. If expert assistance is required, the services of a competent licensed professional should be sought. The author and publisher shall have neither liability nor responsibility to any person or entity with respect to any loss or damage caused, or alleged to be caused, directly or indirectly, by the information contained in this book.

Cover Design & Layout:
Steve Wilson
Insight Publishing
www.insightpublishing.com

*Dedicated to
my honey of a husband
who laughs with me regularly,*

Phil L. Donihe

Laughing Together

Your personality as a couple may already include lots of laughter. However, you may have become a little too serious. Changing this pattern does not mean pursuing social activities simply to fill your time. It can include finding humor in your everyday lives, deepening your friendship, and pursuing what you enjoy doing together.

Laughter, humor, and uplifting time together as a couple and with others can benefit you physically, mentally, emotionally, and spiritually in some of these ways:

- Improve your health
- Increase your energy and productivity
- Add balance to your lives and tranquility to your minds
- Relax and prevent you from taking yourselves too seriously
- Improve the ability to cope with difficulties
- Increase the strength of your friendship
- Deepen your emotional and physical intimacy
- Encourage and assist each other with personal growth and change
- Increase harmony, unity, and relationship satisfaction
- Prompt gratitude for your lives, relationship, and family

Humor, happiness, and joy are part of a balanced life. Laughter is contagious. It spreads to lift the spirits of one another and out to family members, friends, and acquaintances. Compatible humor, shared laughter, and fun times contribute to staying together as a couple.

Staying Together

I'm not perfect
Neither are you
But when we laugh together
It creates couple glue
In our moments of fun
We still say, "I choose you"!

Table of Contents
Some Ways to Laugh Together and Stay Together

1. Pay close attention when arriving and leaving.
2. Look after your well-being before communicating.
3. Notice when to be supportive.
4. Enjoy physical touch and loving actions.
5. Lighten up when issues arise.
6. Be good friends.
7. Smile and let your inner happiness show.
8. Create laughter with play and teasing.
9. Honor the uniqueness in each other and in others.
10. Nurture your loving connection.
11. Include family and friends.
12. Appreciate the good in one another and in your lives
13. Imagine the possibilities of your futur-together.
14. Raise one another up to a higher level.
15. See the long view.

-1-

Pay close attention when arriving and leaving.

"You don't have to say 'Hi' every time we pass each other!"

Remember to be flexible and fun in creating connections.

-2-

Look after your well-being before communicating.

Remember to prepare physically, mentally, emotionally, and spiritually before speaking about anything important.

-3-

Notice when to be supportive.

"Today I got a tatoo on my lower back -- instructions for giving me a great back rub!"

Remember to give kind and thoughtful service to one another.

-4-

Enjoy physical touch and loving actions.

"Knock it off, Hon -- I'm trying to read!"

Remember to deepen your intimacy.

-5-

Lighten up when issues arise.

"I do so share my deepest emotions with you! Hungry and tired are my deepest emotions."

Remember to find and carry out unified solutions.

-6-

Be good friends.

"You changed your Facebook relationship status 347 times today. Want to talk about it?"

Remember to share and compassionately listen to each other's thoughts and feelings.

-7-

Smile and let your inner happiness show.

"I have a big smile on my face, but you can't see it because it's hidden behind a really bad day."

Remember to help each other when life is difficult.

-8-

Create laughter with play and teasing.

"I still love, honor and cherish you...but at my age, I can't do all three at the same time!"

Remember to be kind and loving while having fun.

-9-

Honor the uniqueness in each other and in others.

"I mowed the lawn in a T-shirt for a band that's no longer popular. That's a $75 fine from the Neighborhood Association!"

Remember to share the amusing stories of daily life.

-10-

Nurture your loving connection.

"This is a special night and we'd like everything to be as romantic as possible. On our pizza, could you group the anchovies into couples?"

Remember to spend special time together and in service to others.

-11-

Include family and friends.

"Thank you for calling the Penguin Love Hotline. If your fiancé has cold feet, press 1. If you can't identify your spouse in a crowd, press 2. If fish breath is ruining your mating season, press 3..."

Remember to connect for love, fun, and needed support.

-12-

Appreciate the good in one another and in your lives.

"You grunt a lot better since we took that marriage communication workshop."

Remember to focus on the positive with your thoughts, words, and actions.

-13-

Imagine the possibilities of your future together.

"I would climb the highest mountain and swim the deepest ocean for you...if you let me buy a bunch of cool high-tech gear for the trip!"

Remember to create shared dreams and goals.

-14-

Raise one another up to a higher level.

"That's why God gave us two ears -- one to hear what you say and one to hear what you mean."

© Randy Glasbergen
glasbergen.com

Remember to share your joy and gratitude.

-15-

See the long view.

"And this one is for my greatest achievement – raising a family and staying married for 40 years!"

Remember to count your anniversaries and celebrate being together.

Note of Encouragement

Life has good times and tough times.
It is a gift to be able to look for the humorous
moments in each day and share them,
regardless of what life brings.

Now you have some ideas for physically,
mentally, emotionally, and spiritually
lightening up.
Remember when you laugh together,
you will be more likely to stay together!

About Susanne M. Alexander
www.marriagetransformation.com

Susanne M. Alexander is a Relationship and Marriage Educator, Coach, and character specialist with her education and publishing company Marriage Transformation®. She tends to be serious, so she loves to see how humor and fun strengthen relationships and marriages.

In her life, Susanne has been single, dating, engaged, married, divorced, and widowed. She has been a parent, stepparent, and grandparent. She has also been a child and a stepchild. All of this has given her a diversity of experience to share! She is currently enjoying being married.

Susanne is the author and coauthor of over a dozen books on relationships, character, marriage preparation, and marriage. This is her second cartoon book. Susanne is available as a speaker, workshop leader, and for coaching with clients for individual work and couple assessments before and after marriage for compatibility or strengthening.

About Randy Glasbergen
www.glasbergen.com

Randy Glasbergen is one of America's most widely and frequently published cartoonists and humorous illustrators. His freelance and syndicated cartoons are seen all over the world in newspapers, magazines, greeting cards, books, calendars, advertising, and social media. Randy's comic panel "The Better Half" is syndicated by King Features Syndicate, appearing seven days a week in print and online newspapers around the world since 1982.

Randy's customers include: *Harvard Business Review, Macy's, Hallmark Cards, International Olympic Committee, IBM, China Daily, The Economic Times of India, American Greetings, Dunkin' Donuts, Warner Music Group, Good Housekeeping, United States Postal Service, Ebony Magazine, Reader's Digest, Funny Times, Wall Street Journal, Time Warner Cable, Proctor and Gamble, Chicago Historical Society, Cosmopolitan, Glamour, Bally Total Fitness, Better Homes and Gardens, MasterCard, Oxford University Press, Saturday Evening Post*, and many other publishers, companies, organizations, and universities around the world.

Appreciation

We appreciate the editorial input and commitment to excellence of the following people: Alex Blakeson, Jennifer DeMaria, Phil Donihe, Mioara Gram, Candace Hill, Joyce Teal, David Wright, and the Chattanooga Chatters Advanced Toastmasters Club.

Please contact us at
Marriage Transformation®
for other helpful materials on this theme
and on building and enriching
relationships and marriages generally.

Marriage Transformation®
Susanne M. Alexander, President
www.marriagetransformation.com
susanne@marriagetransformation.com
423-599-0153

www.ingramcontent.com/pod-product-compliance
Lightning Source LLC
Chambersburg PA
CBHW070038040426
42333CB00040B/1721